Nicole,
Snuggle don't
struggle

...THE **LONGING** OF THE **BRIDE**

ERIC WILLIAM GILMOUR

Lovesick: The Longing of the Bride

ISBN: 1724785516
ISBN-13: 978-1724785510

Pulpit to Page Publishing Co. books may be ordered through booksellers or by contacting:

Pulpit to Page Publishing Co.

Warsaw, Indiana

pulpittopage.com

Dedication

Oh Lover of My Soul, You are all to me. You are all I desire to see. All that I desire to know; all that I long for and all my enjoyment. Precious Righteous One standing before God on my behalf and the source of any standing in righteousness I might have. Thank you for your blood and Spirit. Wonderful Trinity take all of me.

Words of Love

"There is only one reality.

I love you.

It doesn't matter that your heart is small.

I will expand it, but let it all be Mine.

Love Me alone!

I will attend to maintaining you.

If you will but dwell in Me, that which is in the Vine will also be in the branches.

What is it that I require?

Love, only love, for he who loves Me, serves Me.

Oh love Me more- Oh much more!- than human beings love one other.

Let go of all that is not necessary to you-all that does not lead you directly to Me, so as to be altogether Mine."

—Jesus to Mary of the Holy Trinity/Josepha Menedez/Consolata Betrone

"God comes to me in silent hours, as morning dew to summer flowers."

—Mechtild von Magdeburg

Contents

Introduction

I am deeply inadequate to write on the holy theme of a lovesickness, shared between the bride and the Perfect Bridegroom. I would never be so arrogant as to assume that I could ever fully understand these holy mysteries.

However, I do believe that if the reader, with humility and wholeheartedness, would receive the invitation that God will make through these pages, they will experience something that will far exceed anything that I could ever hope to articulate in this short book.

My prayer is that you find a "secret unction" hidden under these words that will compel you to taste and enjoy the Bridegroom in way far beyond your wildest imagination of holy romance. As God's ultimate desire is to dispense His own Life into His creatures through communing with the words of His Heart, I am convinced that God will lavish His perfect love upon you through this unlearned and foolish heart of mine.

In recent weeks, my heart felt that "holy itch" to write again but I had no idea what He wanted me to write; so, I waited. Oh precious ones, did you notice that last sentence?

Waiting is the divine sifting in which God can remove the dross-filled desire for attention, significance and the terrible plague of human reasoning that offers to God things that are so contrary to His nature that He cannot, and never will, accept them.

Waiting pulls the Whisper of the Bridegroom toward the ear of our soul. Friends, when we really understand its significance we know that waiting is the difference between Saul and David and between Ishmael and Isaac. Why is waiting so severe and difficult? The issue of waiting is the issue of origin. Origin is everything. Actions rooted in human might and sight will never delight God.

If His glory is the aim of all our aims, then waiting is our way. The wonderful lovesickness in the story of Jacob and Rachel reveals the beautiful picture of love between Christ and His bride. Seven years of hard labor failed to dampen the yearning in his heart for her. He would accept nothing less; it had to be Rachel.

He could have settled for something less with Leah, satisfied with the idea of taking a bride. But, he refused! So it is with a heart that loves Him enough to wait on Him. I am not content to have something like You or something related to You.

I want you, Lord. I can hear John Kilpatrick in my heart, "I want you. I don't want religion. I don't want another church. I don't want another congregation. I don't want another bible. I don't another wife, I don't want more kids. I want you Lord!

Something in the deep part of me is crying out! The Holy Spirit is trying His best to introduce the body of Christ to the Living Bridegroom. But it seems to me that our heart is set on everything else but Him. You see it is not about falling on the floor. It is not about preaching. It is not about evangelizing. It is not about pasturing. It is not about buildings. It is not about money. It is about the Lord Jesus Christ."

Dear reader, Jesus. Jesus alone! His presence! Just Him. Only Him. Precious Bridegroom captivate our hearts again! As I waited for a few months before writing a word, pushing away the urge simply to fill a page with truths and clever articulations, God met me in a wonderful way. This life-changing personal experience is what has birthed these pages. You might ask; what does your personal experience have to do with my life? I know that God's nature is to take the words herein that He has spoken into me, and the experiences that He has thrust upon me, to pull you into a greater, more profound experience of His Son.

Whether you are thriving in God or barely surviving in God, this lovesick treatise will aid the health of your soul. To borrow the words of A.W. Tozer, "the flame in my heart may not be large but it is real. And there may be some who can light their candle with its flame."

Pray this with me. "Precious Living Bridegroom, make Yourself audible to my heart, tangible to my spirit and visible to my soul that I may love you more than I do now."

CHAPTER ONE

Lovesick

"…I am lovesick."
Song of Songs 2:5

Nearly three weeks before writing this, I experienced an intense season of "sickness of love." I use the word "intense" simply because, for my poor soul, it was nothing short of extreme. What I am about to describe may not seem "intense" to another but what I write, nonetheless, is an attempt to convey, from my heart, even to the smallest degree, what sometimes happens in the life of someone who seeks to live in holy lovesickness.

During this time of extreme lovesickness, my stomach felt constantly sick, not physically, but deep inside my soul existed a rumbling that I could only describe as Life swallowing death. Although it did not physically hurt, butthere was what I can only describe as a sort of inward bleeding. It was akin to a "spiritual bereavement", coupled with a strange consciousness and desire for God so overwhelming that I was unable to eat. Bereavement can be defined as an irretrievable loss of something held dear.

This is the best way to describe it. I was without appetite and nothing passed through my mouth for days. Yet it was nothing like fasting. Fasting is intentional and dedicated to God. This was not that. This simply happened to me. I did not schedule it. It merely happened; He seized me to Himself.

During these days, I also could not sleep through the night. I would wake up, caused by the overwhelming sense of God's love and presence, cry for a little while, and then go back to sleep only to have this experience repeated several times each night. I couldn't function because I was in a constant state of ecstatic meditation/adoration that brought with it a deluge of love and the inebriating consciousness of Him into my soul.

I can hear the famous words of St. Ignatius, "Oh Blood of Christ, inebriate me!" When these times of intensity first started happening to me, I learned quickly that blissful adoration is the lover's wonderful state of being.

For nearly a week there was what I can only describe as the sense of an "irretrievable loss of something that I had held dear." Though I do not know exactly what it was that had been ripped out of my inward being, I know enough to say that its residence in my heart provoked the fiery flash of God's jealous love for me.

When my wife went through a similar season she noted, "It seems I am mourning a death of some kind. And I guess I am mourning a death…my own." So it was with my soul. I wept constantly. The hallways, kitchen, living room, car, my closet and pillows were wet with tears; tears from a broken heart aching for God. The Psalmist writes of such a craving using the words, "My soul pines for you." What an incredible string of words. Think of the meaning of these words.

My soul (all that I am) is pining (literally aches) for nothing other than You. It was St. Teresa of Avila who explained this pinning as, "my soul suffers out of desire for Him." Lovesickness in the soul may, at times, be accompanied with seasons of intensified acute aching, throbbing with love and longing to simply groan, gaze and adore. Many of you reading thing know exactly what I experienced. I pray that as you read this description it would remind your heart of some of your own wonderful seasons of intense love exchange with Him.

Though these were days full of random emotional breakdowns in which I was overcome with such a love craving for Him that I looked as if I lost my dearest loved one, they were also permeated with blissful currents of what felt like a river of honey flowing over, in and around me. I am not sure what was actually happening to me. But somehow I know these were deep workings of the Spirit in my soul. What they performed in my heart was more than a million years of exhaustive theology or the self-imposed "chiseling of spiritual disciplines."

Forgive my redundancy, but all that I do know is that my heart was aching with love for Him whose heart aches for us. "Deep calls unto deep" is the language that comes to mind. To one degree or another such aching should be a part of our lives. This is lovesickness. He calls us closer.

He beckons us upon the waters of His love. He whispers to come away to the wilderness where no other voice can be heard. Close your eyes for 10 seconds and listen with your heart, whoever and wherever you are.

St. John of the Cross once wrote, "When one walks lovesick for God…he is at the heights of prayer life and he is fulfilling the great command to perfection." How precious the lovesick life is and how wonderful are these kind of intense seasons where spiritually deep things can be worked into the yielded soul. Don't feel discouraged if you are unfamiliar with what I am talking about. I am aware that though lovesickness is the bride's way of life, the intensity of seasons like the one I just passed though are uncommon to most people. But one thing is undeniably true; such seasons are for available to everyone. This is why you are holding this book. He beckons you.

I also know that these times of great intensity are periodic. Why? Simply because such a state of broken heartedness that robs sleep and appetite makes it impossible to sustain a marriage, a family, a job or even physical life. This is not God's desire. His desire is to seize you to Himself and make you a fountain of grace for your family and those you come into contact with.

Shakespeare once penned a brilliant string of words expressing a lover's deep sickness of love for another. He wrote, "How weary, stale, flat and unprofitable seem to me all the things of this world." Such a sickness of love is a desire so intensely singular that it is unable to be satisfied, content or to even experience moments of happiness apart from the loved one. To apply these words to the case of holy love-sickness, it is a Spirit produced love eruption in the soul such that it is unable to enjoy anything independent of God. For the Lovesick, any enjoyable thing must first pass through Him.

I recall the words of the deceased prophet Arthur Katz, "Jesus refused any fulfillment or gratification independent of His Father." Jesus – perfect lovesick Son that He was – shows us the glistening morning dew resting on His head as He daily chose the place of solitude with His Father. He was drawn, literally inwardly pulled by love, to rest upon His Father and have every element of His life issue from that quiet place of solitude. This is the only place in which the lovesick heart finds enjoyment and consolation, "let His left hand be under my head and His right hand embrace me." To experience the bosom of the Father is Life itself and to remain there is perfected godliness. That inexplicable craving to lay upon His chest is lovesickness. Holiness is simply the lifestyle of the lovesick. For true holiness can be summed up in statements such as, "I shall not want" or "There is nothing on earth I desire besides You."

The phrase, "lovesick" is found in Solomon's poem of two lovers so set upon having each other that to them the whole world seemed to exist as a stage for their mutual intimate experience. Throughout this poem it seems that even those around them (daughters of Jerusalem) seemed to have their part in pointing these lovers attention back to each other. Oh the lovesick soul sees Him alone. There is a seeing that induces holy blindness.

Richard Rolle writes of the lovesick one, "Other delight and other joy it does not desire, for in this degree the sweetness of Him is so invigorating and enduring, His love so burning and cheering that he or she who is in this can as easily feel…so wonderful I cannot describe it. (The soul is then) loving Jesus, thinking Jesus, desiring Jesus, breathing only in its desire for Him, singing to Him, catching fire from Him, resting in Him. (In this place) your thoughts turn to song and into harmony. Death will seem sweeter than honey, (for by it) you will see Him who you love."

Such words express the same love that we see scripted by the lover's pen dripping with love better than wine in the Song of Solomon. It expresses the sensual and experiential love exchange between two love-stricken, single-eyed persons, whose lives are marked by an overwhelming craving for unbroken union with each other. Lovesickness teaches us that the love exchange with Jesus is too beautiful to give our attention elsewhere. Lovesickness teaches that it is far better to give attention to Him, who causes fruit, than to give attention to the development of any single aspect of fruit. Lovesickness teaches us that the highest of all is in His person alone. Lovesickness is the greatest safeguard against the carnal and all of those religious substitutions for Him. Sometimes we think something is so important. It may be a teaching or a revelation or a perspective, or a ritual or a manifestation of some kind. But whatever it is, it pales in comparison to His person, seen, heard, touched and experienced.

As you read this book, my prayer is that you would feel the breath of His Spirit whispering to your heart as you arrive, anew, at the same abandonment as Martha Kilpatrick described in her book Adoration, """Give some? A part…no it must be all, for He is all to me."

CHAPTER TWO

Open to Me

"Open to me… My Darling."
—Beloved to the Love, Song of Songs 5:2

I don't think there is a clearer phrase that conveys God's desire for His people to yield to Him than these three words, "Open to Me…" This may seem elementary, but, for Him to say such a thing to us indicates that we are responsible for His entrance. The sad fact is that in one way or another we are always finding ways, directly or indirectly, to shut Him out. What do I mean? I mean that we choose to go on in His things, His language, His power, His purpose, His gifts, His family, His realm, while no longer looking to Him as our source and center. In order for our Christianity to be "in Christ", everything must emerge from and through the presence of Christ. Whether intentional or not, many of us live totally unaware of His presence. It never dawns on us that He mourns over our lack of awareness of His presence.

It never even crosses our minds that He is waiting for us, always ready, willing and longing to be all to us. Maybe it is because we think that this figurative "door that needs to open" that "separates us" is on loose hinges and seems to close the moment you take your foot out from under it. We all tend to be easily distracted from Him. I know this about myself; I am forgetful. I am consistently confronted with many issues that stir my self-consciousness so I get sidetracked and, consequently, my heart becomes hardened from the ease and simplicity of giving Him my attention. I know that if I am to receive Him through communing with Him I must first be open to Him. And if I am ever to open to Him, it follows from turning my attention to Him.

In Revelation, Chapter 3, we see the same picture of "Open to Me." Here lives the same cry of the Bridegroom. "Behold, I stand at the door and knock, if any man hears my voice and opens the door, I will come in to him and will dine with him and he with Me."

Why do you knock on someone's door? You may answer, "so that they will let you in." True, but that follows something easily overlooked but extremely important.

The first reason you knock is to get the ATTENTION of the one inside.

Why does God knock? It is to let us know that He is here. All He wants is our attention to be pulled from everything else and given to Him. The issue with our souls is that there are so many things that try to compete with Him; our needs, wants, frustrations, hurts, decisions that need to be made and so on. But each of these must be abandoned if we are going to set our hearts to adoring Him. Oh dear reader, you who have struggled to find the sweet abiding presence of God, if you get quiet and listen, you can hear Him, even now, whispering, "I am here. I am here. Open to Me, My love. Let me in." The omnipresence of the Lord (the fact that He is always with you) shows us that the ultimate sin, self-consciousness, is living moment-to-moment unaware of His presence.

Jesus is looking through the door, reaching His hand through whatever opening there may be, so that we might see Him. He loves for us to perceive Him. He hopes that if we can even slightly perceive Him as He reaches for us, He might arouse our desire to experience His love in communion with His person and presence. Jesus knocks. Jesus speaks.

Jesus reaches – "give Me your attention. Respond to My presence. Open to Me." Oh dear reader - who is not yet convinced of our dire need to perceive God - the implanted faculty of our spirit at our new birth is the very means by which He perceptibly communes with us, exchanging love with us, and setting up His rule in our hearts. Jesus is showing us that through this He can become our life-supply.

The ease of simply yielding to Him is only a reality in those who have first given their attention to His knocking. I have seen that many, if not all of us, seem to be like this, whether we will admit it or not. We allow this or that to distract us.

Even if we do turn our attention to Him many of us let things stand between us and simply opening the door to let Him in. It is extremely heartbreaking to think of the wounded Son of man and Lover of our souls "standing behind our wall…looking…peering through the lattice." As Julian of Norwich wrote in a vision of the Lord, "…he waits for us…mourning..." He peers through the lattice of our own pride and knowledge - our own "spirituality" and stubbornness - our inattentiveness and arrogance turns us away from His humble person.

Can you hear His whisper, seeking to let us know that He is here, longing for us to, "Open to Him"? Maybe you don't see the Lord in this way. But the humiliation and suffering on the cross is enough to show His tender heartedness towards you. Each drop of blood fell from that cross creating a symphony of His love for you.

As He hung there, His open arms pleaded with all to open to Him. Each day we must remember the openness of the Bridegroom calling to our hearts to open to Him. I remember I was in a store shopping with my wife and a song came on over the intercom. It was called "A Thousand Years." The lyric "I have died every day waiting for you" shot through me like a holy love arrow.

I went to the restroom shut the stall door and wept, I was touched by His Spirit showing me that the death of Christ daily speaks, "open to me, I am waiting for you." Just as He cannot take back His death, He has forever extended the desire of His heart for our hearts to open to Him. The communion elements are a reminder of His waiting and invitation for us to come to Him in the midst of all of our filthiness. He knows that we are wicked and that we have great difficulty in taking our eyes off of ourselves. It is this very weakness that attracts Him to us. We simply need to recognize our deep-seated depravity and cast ourselves upon Him. Even now as you read this book, see Him; hear Him. The Bridegroom's cross is the certainty of His daily waiting for you.

You may think that you have shut Him out too many times. You may think that He couldn't possibly still want you in the same way He did the first time He knocked. Oh dear reader, you misunderstand the way He is. You fail to realize the Bridegroom's tender heartedness towards His Bride. He longs for you. He looks at you. He waits for you. His knock is not restricted, for Jesus says, "if any man…"

The invitation goes out to all. The invitation goes out to you. Right now, in the midst of your issues, in the midst of your stress, in the midst of your brokenness there is a divine table that descends from heaven spread for you, for any, for whoever will yield and let Him in. "Come, ye poor afflicted ones, who groan beneath your load of wretchedness and pain, and you shall find ease and comfort! Come, you sick, to your Physician, and be not fearful of approaching Him because you are filled with diseases; expose them to His view and they shall be healed. Children, draw near to your Father, and He will embrace you in the arms of love! Come, you poor, stray, wandering sheep, return to your Shepherd! Come sinners, to your Savior! (Madame Guyon)."

Maybe your question is "How do I open to Him?" or what does it even mean to "Open to Him"? It is encapsulated in a single word, surrender. Some might use the word, yield. Let me give an example of the hindrances to surrender or yielding. This may serve as a better description of what it means to yield than even the clearest definition.

Many times, publically, we begin to sense the moving of the Lord upon our hearts and immediately think, "If I give myself to this, I don't know what is going to happen to me. I am not sure what it will look life. What will people think of me?" or we say to ourselves, "Why here? Why now? Could we do this later?"

Many times, when we are alone, some of us can sense Him behind the door of our hearts saying, "Open to Me" and we will approach the door by recognizing that He is near but we will do everything short of actually letting Him in. We hold ourselves back from Him. We may acknowledge Him. We may press up our ear against the door but contact will only happen when you cross the point of no return and open to Him. He will give Himself to those who cast off all reservation and yield themselves to Him.

Whether in public or in private, we must realize that the disposition of yielding is the same whether you are in a public place or a private place. The sense of His presence is His knocking on the door but, to open to Him, we must yield, then and only then will He come in.

For some the resistance is fear; we are scared of what He will do to us. We are afraid that He may alter us in some way that would rob us of some cherished pleasure or aspect of our personality. For some reason we think He will take something that we love from us. He is not that way. We often fear to give things up to Him out of a fear for their safety. But nothing is safe that is not committed to Him.

We must realize that only if He is everything can He safely give us anything. He is the ultimate pleasure and any cherished thing apart from Him is inferior. God animates your personality. The Spirit enhances every pleasure. But, oh dear reader, if there is something that He must take from you He takes it to spare you from the deadly effects of an "uncleansed love" and replaces it with the ultimate satisfaction of Himself. He will always lavish Himself upon those who come to Him. "Surely God would not have created us to be satisfied with nothing less than His presence if He had intended that we should go on with nothing more than His absence (AW Tozer)." In the words of Paul the apostle in Romans 8:32, "He that spared not His own Son, but delivered Him up for us all; how shall He not, with Him, freely give us all things?"

Whatever our hesitation is to opening ourselves to the presence of the Heavenly Bridegroom, it originates in an unwillingness to forfeit self-consciousness. Let me give a example through a story.

Earlier this year I was at a conference in Houston, Texas where I was called to introduce a dear friend. I had been unable to stop crying during worship because of a deep sense of God's presence. Noticing this, the host of the night said to me, "Before you introduce our brother, let them know what has been happening to you." As soon as I started to speak I could feel an intensification of the presence of the Bridegroom. At first I was wondering what the Lord was doing, while also trying not to reveal that there was such an overwhelming sense of God inside of me. I thought to myself, "What if I am the only one who feels this right now? What if I give in to this and I look like a total fool because of the timing and lack of "spiritual atmosphere" amongst the people right now? After all I am supposed to introduce another."

At that moment I blurted out, "If you will yield to Him in the way that He is moving on you, He will be able to come into that area and perform a deep work in your heart. But on the contrary, if you do not yield to Him, He cannot perform that work." I said, "You have to forget about yourself and everyone else...To yield is to say with all of your heart, I do not care what other people think or what happens to me, come in Lord and do whatever you want to do to me." The moment that those words came out of my mouth, the Lord placed a question before me. "Even if they do not open to Me, will you?"

I saw Him with the vision of my soul, standing at the door of my own heart asking me to value Him more than my appearance before respected men and woman of God. "Open to Me," He whispered. I froze. As I vacillated between yielding and not yielding 3 seconds felt like 3 hours. And with the simplicity of giving up, I caved in at His feet and broke down to a sobbing mess. Once I inwardly threw off all restraint and pride and self-consciousness a rush of love hit my whole being like a title wave and I began to cry from so deep within that felt I would vomit. Currents of God flooded my body over and over. People began to come from all over the meeting and get on their faces before God and weep. Needless to say, God performed a deep work in my heart that night. I still feel the effects of it to this day.

It is important to note that had I not yielded, surrendered and opened to Him, it would have altered much more than just that night. I would be different today. Not to say that another opportunity would never have come, but because I yielded and looked like a complete fool in front of thousands, such an abandonment released me to be more His than I otherwise would have been had I kept the door closed and been content to merely hear, but not respond, to the voice of His invitation to a holy love exchange.

Even as you read this now, I beg you on behalf of the Lord; do not be content just to sense the invitation. Don't be content to merely hear the knocking of His holy hand upon the door of your heart. Yield; open to Him. He is your loving Bridegroom. Yes, just put the book down and with all sincerity and vulnerability of heart say, "Please, come in my Precious Lover. Precious Jesus, don't wait outside, come live in me. Make me Your home today and always." If you will daily give Him time to come in, I promise, He will daily sweep you off your feet and hold you in a way that will heal and fill your soul in areas you didn't even know needed healing and filling. His touch will forever damage you beyond repair. He will unite Himself with your soul in a highly experiential way. I am learning over and over that in yielding we may look like fools, but that is the life of the lovesick. A holy Bride is wholly His.

For those of you who are unfamiliar with what I am saying, let me practically talk you through this.

Abandon all other things and turn the gaze of your soul upon Him. Once you sense the slightest impression from His Spirit, cast off all restraint and cast yourself upon Him in absolute trust. Let Him take you; whether you are in a service, a meeting, the kitchen, or in your closet. These impressions are a heightened sense of awareness of His person through which you may pass into Him and Him into you. It is a union, an entrance into one another, a moment that carries your heart into fresh perceptions of Him. Most often, these precious sweet impressions will happen to you in times of waiting in His presence. But if they take place anywhere else, or at any other time, there is a reason. Let me encourage you, above all, do not resist Him. For stubbornness deteriorates our hearts. The definition of stubbornness is, "A resolute adherence to one's one will."

Yielding is laying your will at His feet; the resolute adherence to His will. As Madame Guyon wrote, "we cannot arrive at divine union without the repose of the will." While stubbornness says to the Lord, "I do sense You, but I am not going to let You carry me out of myself, nor out of my own controlled presentation of myself." This is why Jesus, as well as Stephen, rebuked the Pharisees. A "stiff-necked people" are a people who will not yield. The slightest yielding to the Spirit will bring about more experiential knowledge of God's person than a lifetime of theological study or ascetic discipline. For the issue is, and has always been, the heart, "Do not harden your heart" but rather open your heart to Him in whatever way He chooses to come, just receive Him.

I once read advice from an old Christian saint of God who shook America with the power of God, "Cherish the slightest impressions of the Spirit." This is the secret of increase. Dear reader, yielding to the sweet impressions of the Spirit is the best way to cherish God Himself. Cherishing Him is the greatest stewardship of Him. This is what separates the men from the boys. The greatest saints are not those who have fasted the most, or those who know the most, or those who are loudest or most entertaining but, rather, those who have learned the beautiful death of attentiveness and surrender to God. Those who can sing back to the Lord, "I have died everyday waiting for you."

I have been in meetings where the people literally refused to yield to God. I have been in events where people stubbornly stood there in arrogant self-righteousness or super spirituality. People whose attitude is, "I know this already" or "Who are you to teach me?" or "You don't know the encounters I have had." We must cast all that away and say, "I know there is more of you to have and I want it."

I have also been in meetings where the people where literally waiting for the first mention of the name of Jesus so that they may throw themselves at His feet. It is no wonder that, upon my return a year or so later, the most developed ones were those who chose to yield while the others are either backslidden or enclosed in their tower of arrogance. When God poured out His Spirit in Pensacola, Florida in 1995 one of the most interesting things about the move of God was the effects of the Spirit in the people. Night after night the people were touched by God and to this very day I have yet to see a people more all-out obsessed with God; hungry for His presence and preparing to meet the Bridegroom.

If we choose to yield to Him, He will fill us and simultaneously expand our capacity for yielding. I can't help but feel that each of us stand upon the brink of breaking into new realms of God's glorious person. We have as much of God as we want, for He always gives Himself freely to all. They only thing needed is for a person, any person, anywhere to say – "I don't give a rip what anyone thinks of me or what happens to me, I will go away with you, I will open my heart and yield my entire being to the movement and work of your Spirit."

CHAPTER THREE

Kisses of God

"Let Him kiss me with the kisses of His mouth."
Song of Songs 1:2

One of the most beautiful ways to describe an experience is the word, "kiss." It suggests loving and intimate contact. It is tender. It is face-to-face. To borrow language from Bernard of Clairvaux, "the kiss…is a participation in the life and love of the Trinity." John 1.3 tells us that "our fellowship is with the Father, and with His Son Jesus Christ." He also tells us that this fellowship is the very reason why he is proclaiming the Word of Life to them (1 John 1.3). Likewise, Paul tells us that this fellowship is experienced by the Spirit (2 Cor. 13.14). Oh highest wisdom! Oh tender love! To be kissed by you! To gaze upon you! Oh, How beautiful! The kiss is the Bride's source of life. The kiss is the Bride's inclusion into the divine Trinitarian fellowship. Bernard expounds upon this divine

Kiss, "…if anyone receives the Spiritual kiss of Christ's mouth he seeks eagerly to have it again and again. It is hidden manna (Rev. 2.17), and he who eats it hungers no more. It is a…fountain and he who drinks from it thirsts for…Him alone."

And furthermore, "When we are joined with Him in holy kiss we are made one with Him in Spirit through His kindness." In which one, "…finds rest in Him in the rapture which is the kiss of His mouth." As the great shinning sun swallows the lesser lights in the sky, so the kiss of God will diminish all other desires and perpetually be our magnificent obsession. "Let those who have experienced the Kiss enjoy it. Let those who have not experienced the Kiss, burn with desire, not so much as to know it but to experience it (Clarivaux)."

The enjoyment and bliss of the Bride is to live a life of intimate receptivity.

"Let Him Kiss me…" It is important to note that the Bride's disposition is one of yielding, not action. She does not say, "I am gonna kiss Him." As Madame Guyon once wrote concerning the experience of God, many times, "activity obstructs union." As the "smothered fire must be gently fanned; but as soon as it is kindled, we must cease that effort, lest we extinguish it by our own activity." With such a surrendered heart the Bride rightly says, "Let Him kiss me…" The word "let" means permission. God waits not for the perfection of the life; He waits only for the consent of the heart. He knows you are powerless to change yourself. He also knows the power of His own kiss upon your life. Therefore He waits for the consent of the soul and He will rush in like a love-drunk bridegroom to rescue and thrill our heart with His kiss. Oh here is a good place to stop and quietly say, "Jesus, I love you."

Dear reader, can you sense the gravity of His kind invitation "Drink and imbibe deeply, O lovers." It is easy to read over this statement and think it to be only a poetic string of words, thereby missing the wonderful truth hidden therein. To drink Him is to love Him. To love Him is to drink Him. For drinking is the lover's union. Drinking Him is receiving Him. The drink is a kiss and the kiss is a drink.

This intoxicating love exchange, is likened to wine, "for Your love is better than wine." Immediately following the kiss it is written, "The King has brought me into His chambers." A kiss, a drink, a love exchange with Him who now pulls you alone into His bedroom! Solitude is the lover's chamber and wine will always be the beverage of the Bride. Oh the public kiss turns to a private touch and the Bride passes into the realms of glorious joyful perceptions of Him. Oh the lovesick know these realities and their souls salivate for them again and again.

The Bride says, "How handsome You are my beloved and so pleasant." Her exclamation seems too formal for one who has been brought into the chambers of the King. Let us look at what she is really saying.

She exclaims, "How handsome…" This word means, "attractive or majestic." The word majestic means, "having impressive beauty." It is non-negotiable that "attraction" and "impression" indicate "perceptibility." She is, at the very least, seeking to convey that the vision of Him is extremely perceptible and lovely. She then says, "…and so pleasant." Pleasant word means "enjoyable." He is her enjoyment.

The undeniable characteristic of the Bride is an ineffable enjoyment in the Bridegroom. His presence, His voice, His realm, His person - yes, the heaven of heaven is truly, the

Bridegroom Himself. To bring this all together; her experience of Him has proven His powerfully attractive beauty. She exclaims, "Your whole being is breathtaking!"

If you are having a hard time understanding how this translates to Spiritual relationship with God, let me illustrate. The first time that I ever saw the Lord I tried my best to write in my journal a description of what I saw, heard and felt. I combine all three because I am not sure which one it actually was. He was unadulterated sensory overload.

My words, pen and paper are merely a feeble attempt to explain our soul's magnetic attraction to God. I wrote, "…upon what seemed like seeing Him, in that very instant every one of my desires were pulled toward Him. I was stricken breathless by the overwhelming conviction that He was unlike anything that I have ever seen before. The only thing that I could say through my tears and groaning was, "I do not want to live (here) anymore. Take me with You." For me it was the ultimate Maranatha experience. The Spirit in the Bride truly aches for His return (Rev. 22.17). Let me put this in perspective; I have a beautiful wife and two lovely daughters. My family and life are blessed and I am deeply thankful for these naturally unparalleled joys in this life. But I want to explain that the vision of Him was so magnetic that I wanted to forfeit all of it and everything in this life, forever, to simply always have Him in this capacity. Now, I know that is not at all what He wants from us and I apologize for the weakness of words, but I must at least attempt to convey the meaning of the phrase, "How attractive and enjoyable You are." He is the gravitational pull to our being.

If you pick up a rock and drop it, it is pulled toward the ground. So it is with the soul and the magnetic force towards God. He will pull it to Himself entirely. The only reason our soul will not come to Him is tolerated obstructions. If you pick up the same rock and drop it to the ground with a table under it, it will not hit the ground but stop at the tolerate obstruction. Idols and inordinate affections act as that tolerated obstruction to our vision of God and our pull toward Him. This is why John, who describes God as light and fellowship with God as walking in the Light, writes, "guard yourselves from idols-anything that would take God's place in your heart."

When we see the magnetic pull of God's glorious beauty we can understand why it is written, "rightly do they love you." In other words, "I have seen You and I totally understand how You can capture someone's heart with one glimpse." He who has seen says, "all should love you. It is right to do so." When we truly see His beauty we recognize that it is wrong to not desire Him. It is the ultimate sin for He is the ultimate beauty. In fact, all sin is a gaze away from Him. Idolatry is placing something in front of your gaze upon Him. It is a fixation upon a beauty that is far inferior to Him.

Oh dear reader, why write such things? I write them because God wants you to know that His kisses are for you. The exhilarating love of God is yours to have, to experience and to live by. His attractiveness is the antidote to this world's glitter and our personal selfishness. To see Him and hear Him, to sense Him and be with Him is the inebriating bliss of life. The fruit of which is real life giving holiness. Holy living is the unobstructed Holy One. This is why He died, to give Himself to you.

The New Covenant is the romance of the ages. Loving Him is the root of the Covenant. It reveals to us that the lack of a love experience of Him was, and continues to be, the root of our rebellion. Hence the blood that split the veil, makes a way for us to enter a face-to-face lover's exchange with Him; a lovesick blindness. The rent veil makes way for the Holy kiss. The cross opens to us the ability to surrender our lives to the kiss, the drink, and to, once again, enjoy the touch of the Lover of our souls. What else is worth living for? The true bride wants Him for Him alone. If we come to Him merely to obtain something we are not seeking Him but using Him. But in the words of Mother Basilea Schlink, "You are here. What more could I want?"

Few saints have touched my heart like those who write of Spiritual oneness with God. To close out this chapter enjoy this excerpt from The Spiritual Espousals by John Ruusbroec.

"When Christ has risen as high as possible in our hearts, that is, above all His gifts…God draws the heart, the desires, and all the powers of the soul upward…I cannot easily explain this attraction and invitation…but it consists in the fact that God is inviting and calling the heart to its higher unity with Him.

This interior invitation is more pleasant than anything else that it has ever experienced. Here the heart opens wide, in joy and desire, and all the veins dilate, and the powers of the soul stand ready in their desire to fulfill what is called for by

God. This invitation consists in the shining of Christ, the eternal Son upon the heart. This causes so much pleasure and joy within the heart and makes the heart open so wide that it can scarcely be closed again. A person thereby is wounded in his heart from within and feels the wound of love. Being wounded by love is both the sweetest feeling and the sharpest pain that anyone can experience. The spiritual wound causes pleasure and pain at one and the same time."

CHAPTER FOUR

Solitude

"In His shade I took great delight and sat down, and His fruit was sweet to my taste."
Song of Songs 2:3

Lovers love to be alone. They instinctively seek retreat. A retreat in which no other voice is heard and no other face is seen. A retreat in which the intimate sight and sound thrills every part of the soul with sweetness. For "His mouth is full of sweetness. And He is wholly desirable (Songs of songs 5.16)." Solitude is where we find the expansion and dominance of the inner life. As David Mc'Intyre once wrote, "The equipment for the inner life is simple…It consists particularly of a quiet place, a quiet hour and a quiet heart." The Scripture tells us that "in quietness and trust is our strength (Isaiah 30:15)." Richard Wurmbrand 14 years in communist prison, 7 of them in solitary confinement, taught us that, "The highest form of prayer that

I know is a quiet heart beating that loves Him." The Lover of our souls invites us as the Bridegroom in Solomon's love poem,

"O My dove…in the secret place…let me see your form, let me hear your voice. For your voice is sweet and your form is lovely."

Her heart has the same cry,

"Let us rise early and go (away from here)…there I will give You my love."

We must "…sit alone and be silent…" so as to listen to the Lord (Lam 3.28). We see that David went and "sat before the Lord (2 Sam. 7:18)." The perfect Master understood the same as the source of life for He "went to a secluded place… (Mark1:35)." Solitude was His "custom" (Luke 22:39). The Son of God possessed that lover's aching to "withdraw to lonely places" and find His enjoyment in the Father (Luke 5:16).

It is a peculiar thought, but the depth of yearning between the beloved and the lover is a mutually satisfying thing. As

John Ruusbroec once wrote, "When God pleases us and we please God therein is the practice of love and eternal life." The lovesickness goes both ways, when we receive all our satisfaction from Him this brings satisfaction to Him. What eternal life is and how it is lived out is a matter of man and God enjoying each other. That enjoyment is chiefly found when no one else is around. Lovesickness produces in the soul an endless allurement to solitude.

The reconciliation is nothing short of the restoration of God and man regaining their pleasure in each other. God is somehow satisfied with our love. I do not comprehend this, but it is undeniably appears in the divine image painted by Wisdom's pen. His goal of loving you was to be loved by you. As we look to His glory we are changed through the ultimate blissful union and the resulting satisfaction of His presence and person.

His love flashes with fires of jealousy when we allow other things to take our attention away from Him. For His love for us is "as strong as death" with "jealousy demanding as the grave" and "its flashes are flashes of fire" The very flame of the Lord." Let me give an example of the Bridegroom's jealousy for His Bride's full attention.

I went through a season when an obsession with teachings concerning the Millennial Reign of Christ, little by little, began to take my heart away from experiential communion with God. Though such a truth is correct and is a powerful hope and theme in the New Testament, I had allowed it to steal my attention from His person and presence. Slowly death spread throughout my soul.

But the monstrous substitution that was robbing me of communion began to so deeply blind me that I was unable to see that it was actually draining me. Right in the midst of this time, I received a call from an old friend from bible school who I had not seen in years. God had spoken to him to fly down and spend a few days with me. I was so disconnected internally from the activity of the Spirit that I found it strange that he wanted to visit, but he insisted. So for days he stayed with me. He would spend a half-hour with me and then return to the room in my house where he was staying and pray for a half-hour.

He would come out and hang with me and then return to the room. All day and every day he did this. I have always had a respect for devotion so I was impressed with his constant retreat. I thought his discipline was rooted in taking our appearance before the judgment seat of Christ very seriously, but somehow I could feel that it was more than that, because when he would speak, it was as if his words were alive. Literally, it was as if his voice was living. The Spirit seemed to be tangibly proceeding out of his mouth.

I had lost faith in such things, so I was trying to understand what was really going on. I was so theologically-minded that I weighed every syllable against my mental biblical curriculum. It was very strange to recognize that, though nothing contradicted the plain text, I still had no clue where he was getting such incredibly and undeniably divine truths. He was like a man from another world. His face was the perfect blend of holy meekness and militancy. Everything about his living interaction with God oozed out of him, convicting me deeply, as it showed me that I had lost the most precious thing in my life, communion with God.

So the last night that we were together we were going to hit the streets to preach the gospel. While we were on our way, he said, "Do you have somewhere we can go to be by ourselves and pray together?" I took him to a small prayer chapel with a fountain and air conditioning and we began to pray. All of a sudden without any notice, he turned to me like a living flame of fire and said, "What happen to you?" He just looked at me. Then he continued, "You are not the same." I was angry at his directness and I knew with everything inside me that he was right. With religious, biblical arrogance I quickly searched my mind for a scripture reference to shut him down and build myself back upbut he looked through me and said, "Eric, you need to get right with God." I couldn't think. I couldn't speak.

I simply fell to my knees at his feet crying. There was nothing left to defend myself with. I was defeated by the conviction emanating through the sound of his voice. I had personally left the presence of God and every molecule of my being knew it. He laid his hands on my head as I was at his feet and he said with Holy Ghost authority and power, "God, fill Eric with the Holy Ghost again!"

All that I had forgotten, pushed and reasoned away – all that I had theologically blocked off - happened to me in that very moment. Surges of electric glory went through my being and I was rent in two like the holy veil in the temple and God. God, as light shined through like a violent laser beam reaching into my chest to captivate my heart again. David Popovici was sent by God to save my relationship with the living Christ, to save me from drowning in theology. He personified the flash of the flame of the Lord's jealousy for my heart.

The Lord is burning with jealousy for all of our affection. When my friend David said, "You need to get right with God" it was not a matter of sins or neglect of preaching or study or some secret issue in my life, it was a matter of having forgotten God. I needed to get right with God by returning to a life that lives by and through interaction with Him. There is no other righteousness. To miss Him amidst His things is unrighteousness itself. He will not share the throne of your heart with a principle, a theology, a gift, a friend, a church, self-consciousness or anything else. He burns to have you to Himself. He must always, without hesitation, come before all of His things. The truth is that you cannot "set the Lord before you" if there are other things before Him.

If you have lost your way, this moment He is here looking into your heart. He doesn't look with anger and hatred. He looks with a compassionate selfless heroic love that wants to rescue your heart with His embrace. He is in the room with you now. Turn your heart to Him.

In a similar way, we should feel such burning against those "little foxes" that come in "to spoil the vine" of our pure love exchange with God. It is non-negotiable that the obsession with a full and uninterrupted experience of God creates an addiction to solitude. Not solitude itself, but as a haven in which the greatest pleasures are consumed. The touch, taste, fragrance, sight and sound that we possess through whole-hearted attentiveness to God can make anyplace a "garden of spices."

When God taught men how to pray, He specifically pointed out two things that are essential to our experiencing sweet fellowship with Him. It must not escape our notice that He who fashioned the soul, knowing every detail of its functionality, told us to "go into your closet" and to "shut the door." This is solitude and silence. It is separation and quietness. Hidden inside Christ's golden teaching on prayer is the Lover beckoning us to "come away." The Lover of our souls constantly seeks to pull us away from everything so He can have all of our attention, face-to-face.

Once I woke up in the middle of the night because I felt someone physically grab my chin. It freaked me out. I asked the Lord what it could be and I heard nothing. Until one day,

I was watching my wife working in the kitchen and I was overcome with a romantic love for her and a desire to hold her close and be alone, that I called her to come to me. She didn't listen because she was busy.

It probably wasn't the best time but I just wanted her attention for a minute. When she didn't answer me I simply walked up to her in the midst of all that she was doing and I through my arms around her and forcefully pulled her close. As I playfully held her tightly to restrain her from pulling away from me she was looking over at all the other things she still had to do. I then reached one hand up and gently grabbed her chin and turned her face towards me.

I looked in her eyes and said, "Babe, give me your attention, just for a second." She, playing along, looked at me and said, "Yes, what can I do for you?" I then just continued to look at her without saying a word. I didn't have anything to say I just wanted to receive and give the communication of attentiveness.

It wasn't until after I left the kitchen that the Lord reminded me of when He grabbed my chin in the middle of the night. Now I understood. He just wanted my full attention. He was turning my face towards Him; face-to-face, eye-to-eye, heart-to-heart. He was saying, "Come away with me before the sun rises." I also believe He was telling me that He wants to freshly captivate the hearts of His people with lovesickness again.

If you receive anything from this chapter, let it be that, no matter where you are, He wants you. No matter what has happened or how incredible your pursuit has been, He desires you beyond description. He wants your eyes on Him. He wants your ear on Him. He wants your love on Him. He wants your voice and nearness. "To Him" is always superior to "about Him" and "for Him."

If I know anything about myself, I know that there is something about me that is endlessly degenerative without taking time to simply sit in silence before God. The greatest evidence that we really don't want God to rule our lives is the refusal to sit quietly before Him each day.

Without the empowerment that comes through constant fellowship with God even what we know to be true is empty and powerless and worthless to us and others.

Solomon's poem says the words, "In His shade…" Shade is a shadow. Here is a wonderful truth concerning "drawing near to Him" that He may "draw near to you." Only the divine shadow can block the heat of this life. Such a shadow is cast only upon those who draw near. No one else is mentioned here. The shadow becomes easily perceptible in solitude. In addition he continues, "…I took great delight…" it is in this nearness that we experience the unmatched delight of His person.

One may say, "I am already near to God. I don't think that I can get any nearer." Well, in proximity nothing ever changes, but relationally things easily change. For instance, my wife and I sleep in the same bed. We have a life together in which both of us are involved yet even though in proximity we are always near to each other I may feel that as the years pass by we are growing nearer and nearer.

It is not a matter of position but of relation. Such a growing, knowing and nearness to God is the source of an ever-increasing delight in Him. As Tozer has stated, "The more perfect our friendship with God becomes the simpler our lives will be." I would add, the more delightful our lives will be.

Solomon continues with the image of sitting, he states, "I sat down and his fruit was sweet to my taste." What a beautifully important picture He is painting. A nearness, a delight, a rest and a taste. Notice that the eating takes place after the sitting.

We must learn that rest is the realm of perception. We draw near to Him incomplete shade and delight and then proceed to enter a rest, the ceasing of all activity. Paul's words, "seated with Him" forever unites our union with rest. Man's concept of God is that He desires man for His use, but the bible clearly reveals that God desires man for union. God didn't create man in the garden and present Himself to man as work and sweat, but as rather as a tree to be eaten from.

We must first be fed before we can ever be led. We cannot let our need for leading eclipse our need for feeding. His invitation to man was to receive Him as the source of life. Sweat comes from the striving produced from the lack of the life of God in man's soul.

So it is with the lover's poem; to rest, to taste. She later expounds on such a sweet taste. She reveals the sweetness to be His voice, "His mouth is full of sweetness and He is wholly desirable."

The fact that His voice is sweet means that it is perceptible and not as some suppose; that it exists underneath consciousness. Conscious perceptibility is the most fundamental aspect of communication. The fact that she says the He is wholly desirable explains to us that He attracts every part of our being. He draws us to Him like as a giant magnet, beyond anything that could be perceived in the natural. Knowledge and understanding are said to "come forth from the mouth" of God (Proverbs 2:2).

Consistent with this, the Psalmist says, "How sweet are Your words to my taste! Yes, sweeter than honey." With the mouth men can describe honey, but only the mouth of Jesus dispenses honey. The difference is that teaching and theology will always be inferior to tasting. Proverbs also states, "My Son, eat honey, for it is good, yes, the honey from the comb is sweet to your taste; know that wisdom is thus for your soul."

Notice that it is a command from the Father to the Son to experience the honey. Also notice that it is given to sons to have such an experience. Such a taste is an experience called wisdom. The Scripture shows us all must, "taste and see that the Lord is good,"

It is only in the experience of the sweetness of the Lover that the nature of the Lover can be known. I believe that the lack of the intimate kiss is the source of the misconceptions of God's good nature. It is the satisfaction of that kiss that forms His holy image in our soul.

Knowing God's goodness is not a matter of teaching but of touch. Maybe I can say it this way; Our Lord teaches by touch. In First John 2:27 we are told that the anointing "the smearing" causes us to "know." God's means of teaching us is touching us. He touches us with Himself to teach us of Himself. The things of God that He opens our eyes to in the Scriptures becomes ours and we become them.

As Madame Guyon wrote concerning God's desire to speak Himself into us, "His one will towards His creatures is to communicate Himself unto them." In the wonder of His words, we soon find that Hudson Taylor's words ring true, "There was a music in His voice that awaken echoes in her soul such as no other voice could…"

Dear friends, we need solitude with the Lover of our souls. I am convinced that one moment in solitude with God greatly affects every area of my life. Dear reader, you can take this to the bank, our experience or lack of experience of Him will affect everything.

I have been to countless glorious conferences with many amazing manifestations and power encounters with God, but unless such a public “touch” turns into a private “kiss” it will, in time, fade away. The problem with movements is that it is easy to hide in the lingo, sound, crowds and fad of it all.

And the danger of the intimacy movement is that many have merely adopted the language. But it is the place of solitude and personal communion alone with God that can perform the work that Madame Guyon wrote about, “it delivers us from every vice, and obtains us every virtue; for the one great means to become perfect is to walk in the presence of God.”

Friends, God is very serious about being our One and Only. We must know that any additions, anything other than Him, will soon become extremely poisonous to us.

To spare you the toil of unraveling the old English I have paraphrased a touching story of a preacher talking about his father's life of intimate fellowship with God.

"The home I grew up in was rather small. It consisted of a living room, a bedroom and another room that was extremely small between the other two. It could fit a bed, a small table and a chair. It had an unusually small window through which a little bit of light could shine in. This little room was the sanctuary of our home. Daily and often times throughout the day, generally after each meal, we saw our father retire there and 'shut the door.'

We children had come to know, by a sort of spiritual instinct, that prayers were bring offered up in that room like the Great High Priest Himself behind the veil in the Most Holy Place. We could sometimes hear his quivering voice weeping before God. We learned to tip toe past that door so that we would not interrupt the fellowship he was having with God. The outside world may not know, but we knew, where that happy light came from – like a new born smile that was always shining from our father's face. It was a reflection of the Divine Presence, in the consciousness of which he lived His life."

We must lay upon Him in the place of solitude. We must not merely look in His direction. We must look directly at Him as Moses gave His attention to the burning bush. Tozer has stated, "Inside the center of man's being is a bush where God was meant to glow with moral and spiritual fire."

And Jared Wilson sums all things up nicely by writing, "The essential message of Christianity is not "Behave" but rather "Behold." For fruit is not what man has done for God, but what God has done through man. When a man truly sees God, he becomes blind to all, even the gifts that surround God. If we will put everything else away and look at Him, soon we will forget everything else and receive Him.

More of our soul's needs are met when we are rapt in adoration than could ever be addressed in an endless multitude of prayers. Jesus looked for His Father in order to receive from Him the empowerment for action conveying, "...I only do what I see..." He reveals the essence of sonship with this phrase, "My Father abiding in Me does His works."

Over 50 years ago Tozer pointed out the same, "Jesus' power lay in His continuous look at God." John shows us that Jesus was able to "expound" God because He proceeded from the "bosom" of the Father. The "bosom" of the Father is the source of any revelation of the Father.

Here is an excerpt from an incredible book called, "The Hidden Life of Prayer" written by David McIIntyre that will beautifully and fictionally illustrate to you the solitude in the life of the Lord, the perfect Son.

"In the carpenter's cottage in Nazareth there were, it appears, no fewer than nine persons who lived under the one roof. There were the Holy Child, Mary His mother, and Joseph. There were also the Lord's "brothers" – four of them – and at least two "sisters." The cottage consisted principally of a living room, the workshop and an inner chamber-a sort of closet in which the provision for the day, the kitchen utensils, the firewood, etc., were laid.

That gloomy recess had a latch on the inner -side, placed there, it may be, by the carpenter's Son, for that dark chamber was His oratory, not less sacred than the cloud-wrapped shrine of the Presence in the Temple. Afterwards when our Lord had entered on His public ministry, there were occasions when He found it difficult to secure the privilege of solitude.

He frequently received entertainment from those who showed Him the scantiest courtesy, and afforded Him no facility for retirement. When His spirit hungered for communion with His Father, He was fain to bend His steps toward the rough uplands, "Cold mountains and the midnight air witnessed the sweetness of His prayer…it was His custom to "resort" to the olive-garden of Gethsemane. Under the laden branches of some gnarled tree, our Lord, must often through the soft summer night watch the stars. Any place became a chamber…the soul which turns to God may clothe itself in quietness even in the crowded concourse or in the hurried streets."

CHAPTER FIVE

Direct Contact

"He touched."

Genesis 32:25

The Psalmist wrote of a generation that would, "seek His (God's) face." This phrase follows an interesting connection of words that will help us understand what it means to "seek God's Face." He uses the words "ascend" and "stand." "Ascend" first, and "stand" second. Here the seeking life is defined for us (1) "Ascend," the mountain, which speaks of detachment from all other things, people and places, (2) lingering in God's presence (understood as "standing" in the Holy Place).

He explains what kind of person can and will "ascend" and "stand", or "detach" and "linger," one who has, "clean hands and a pure heart." This is understood to be the absence of a disparity between our lives (hands) and our motives (hearts). At face value one can hardly see the depth of what is really being described; undefiled living and a pure intent in our hearts. It was John Wesley who wrote, "Simplicity is loving intent upon Jesus alone, seeking no other person or thing."

The sad fact is that the seeking of the Lord Himself, namely, His presence and person, above all other things, is a rarity in most Christian circles. Each camp has its interests. One has this gift and another has that gift. One has this emphasis and another has that emphasis. The church has sought gifts, power, miracles, authentic community, relevance, impact, numbers, money, and many other things from God.

Yet, the most important thing, the transformative experience of deeply communing with God Himself, is neglected. God Himself has become a supplement, an afterthought, to His own works. It was John Arndt in the 1500's who wrote, "God Himself and not His gifts are to be our highest desire and joy." And as Tozer penned perfectly, "The full purpose of our salvation is that we might enjoy the manifest, conscious presence of God…when we are enjoying the conscious presence of God, we are fulfilling the tenets of our salvation."

If there is a prayer that is constantly arising in my heart for the church of America and the rest of the world, it is this, that the Lord would revive our gaze upon His face and reveal to us the things we have put in His place.

Only those who look for God alone will detach from everything else and spend time lingering in His presence. This word "linger" touches my heart. For the greatest experiences of Him happen here, in lingering. No pressure to move on or "accomplish" anything, simply lingering with Him with no agenda but His presence. If we will give ourselves to His presence He will give to us His words. It is interesting that the false prophets were rebuked for not "standing in the counsel of the Lord" (Jer. 23.18).

The word for stand is literally understood to be "still." The word for counsel can be understood as "company." The text suggests that the "sweet company" of the Godhead can be perceived in that place of stillness in God's presence. Even the angels of the Lord use the same words, "I am Gabriel, who stands in the presence of God (Luke 1:19)." It would be good to memorize this statement; if we will give ourselves to His presence, He will give to us His words. Receiving the communication of God is the only way to come to know Him personally.

This is why "stillness" is so important. Psalm 46.10 shows us that being "still" brings about the knowing of the I Am. Why? Because being "still" has to do with the abandonment and absence of internal noise and distractions so that God may be heard.

Quietness is the absence of external noise but stillness is the absence of internal noise. It is full attentiveness to God. Those who will detach and linger in His presence will be those who come to know Him. Even as Psalm 46 goes on to note that, "I will be exalted in the earth." This is how God seeks exaltation in the world, through those who will come to know Him. Stillness aids adoration and adoration opens the soul's receptivity to God's presence and His presence is the means of His communication.

But such a life is not the norm these days, far too many of us have accepted turbulence of soul to be the norm and think that it's impractical to find some secret place to gaze upon the beauty of the Lord Himself.

With clean hands and a pure heart, seeking Him, the generation that the Psalmist speaks of will be a people who have nothing to add or acquire from God; a lovesick people fixed upon God Himself for no other reason than God Himself and the fulfillment of His desires through our lives by the receiving His voice. It is interesting that there is a direction that the Psalmist points our attention to when he speaks of such a generation. He points to Jacob. Clean hands? A pure Heart? Not lifting up our souls to vanity or operating in deceit? Jacob? Of all people, why Jacob?

There are many things that come to mind when I think of Jacob. His father; his great desire for the blessing of God that moved him to supplant His brother; his sons; Joseph; his wife; his riches; his service the Bethel ladder. But, for me, all of these pale in comparison to the night of solitude in which his collision with God forever altered his name, life and legacy.

There are many explanations as to why he was drawn to solitude that strange black night, but let none of them take our attention from the simple fact that he was actually alone. Make no mistake about it - solitude is where God makes His man. Solitude is the divine factory of brokenness. Solitude is the chamber of the King. Solitude is a realm in which men can see the invisible and hear the inaudible. Solitude is where man experiences the tangibility, sensibility and edibility of God.

What is brokenness? It is the severe snap and fracture of the resolute adherence to one's own will. Brokenness is the disintegrating of stubbornness and the cause of a humble limp that characterizes the remaining days of that man's life who has been graced with the divine touch of God. Jacob was given a new name to go along with his new limp and so it will be with us.

What was it that brought about such a life-altering fragmentation? If you will forgive my redundancy, I will note again that Jacob was alone. Immediately after the Scripture states that He was alone it states "a Man." The appearance of this Man followed the mention of Jacob's solitude. We find that this "Man" was a manifestation of God. So it is with the beautiful meeting of God and man. It is solitude that aids man in his ability to recognize God.

Here in solitude Jacob recognizes God's presence. In that wonderful recognition of God there is a "wrestling." Beautiful picture it is, yet difficult to understand. There is not another instance like this in all of Scripture. What does this mean…"wrestled with God?" I believe the best way to understand such a wrestling is to understand the most fundamental aspect of any wrestling match and that is direct contact; God apprehending man and man apprehending God.

Paul talks of apprehending that for which God apprehended him (Phil 3.12). God and man engaged in direct contact. If we let this image remain, it is easier to understand what the transforming element of that infamous night actually was. It was in this direct contact that Jacob's "thigh was dislocated." Because of this, he would go on to limp for the rest of his days. So it will be with us. The touch of God will cripple the soul into dependency. Yes, a dependency that will change the way that we walk (live our lives).

Things will be a little slower. Each move will a little more thoughtful, deliberate and important. We will forever lean, unable to stand and walk without the aid of this Innocent Other. Dependency is both the way to allow the Spirit to work and the work of the Spirit. Dependency is a never-ending plunging into the depths of all that God is in us. We must always be careful never to use "spiritual disciplines", fasting or theology as a replacement for simple dependency. Here is wonderful spiritual advice from Andrew Murray, "Expect nothing from yourself but in everything expect and depend upon God." And one of my favorite quotes of all time from the same author, "Remember the one condition, habitually, unceasing absolute dependence on Him."

I remember reading an account about one of the last times a man heard Watchman Nee preach. Paraphrasing, Nee preached an incredible message on brokenness through the story of Jacob's broken hip. In the middle of the message a man stands up in the midst of the congregation and begins to tell everyone that he is a broken man and that his life is limping as evidence.

Nee let the man finish his self-praise and then continued saying, "If a man is truly broken, with a limping life, he will never need to tell anyone. Because the moment that he walks men will see it. But if a man is not truly broken and he tells people that he is broken, he better remember his profession because the moment he forgets everyone will be able to see that he, in fact, has no a limp at all."

My friends, humility is when our legs have been broken by the weight of God's presence. Direct encounter will always leave a man beautifully damaged by God's glory. We cannot fake brokenness; nor can we simply choose to start acting broken. We can only live a life that finds a solitary place where we can recognize God and directly contact Him. Here God can break us. Notice the immediate result when Jacob is broken; he clings to Him. "I will not let You go…"

Thomas Dubay has a masterful statement on the same theme,"…(divine) touch is a deep, intimate-union-experience of God…This contact brings incomparable delight, for in the touch God is sublimely perceived…It is not only a touch but a union." And summarized to perfection, Bernard McGinn writes, "Christianity is that practice that concerns the consciousness of a direct, immediate and transformative encounter with the presence of God." Such a transformation will bleed into every single area of your life. You will never have to tell anyone that you are different, if you are in fact, different.

Those mirroring Jacob's experience are nothing short of a people who are clingingly dependent upon God. Their names have been changed; their literal identity altered by

God. Beware of any "new identity" that has not, at its root, an experience of God's presence in solitude that has shattered a man's stubborn adherence to his own will and causes him to cling to God. Our spiritual maturity is measured by how dependent we are on our perception of God to govern and empower our whole life. We learn dependency behind closed doors. Every truly spiritually developed man will tell you that their spirituality is in exact proportion to the yielding of their soul to God.

CHAPTER SIX

Eating the Bridegroom

"…He who eats Me will live because of Me…"
John 6:57

Dear friends, every word in this book is pointing to the fact that the daily knowing of the Lord requires a daily stillness. As His presence fills us we are convinced that even suffering is inferior to His presence. Absolutely nothing can steal the limitless joys springing up out of a heart that is the dwelling place of God. Just a few days ago a person came to me and asked, "How do I carry the presence of God in my life?" I looked at her and said, "I don't think you will believe me if I tell you." She said, "Please tell me." I said, "The secret to carrying the presence of God is a daily enjoyment of God." She looked at me and said, "Wow, daily enjoyment and what else?" I said, "Nothing else. That is the secret; enjoying Jesus."

So many people are striving to "break something open" all the while failing to enjoy what Jesus has broken open, namely, the veil to between us and the presence of God. These next three words are the some of the most important words anyone can learn about living a life empowered by the Life of God, Arthur Burt said, "snuggle don't struggle." It is in resting upon His breast that we can access the Divine Treasure Chest (Col. 2.3).

Watchman Nee wrote, "If Christ is LIFE then we need to do the work. But if Christ is LIFE then we need not struggle...If there is LIFE, there will not be the slightest need for our own doing but rather that LIFE will naturally flow."" A life of mere spiritual discipline pales in comparison to one moment of receiving His Life through the enjoyment of fellowship with God. We absorb God through enjoying Him. Recently I listened to a popular bible teacher give an overview of the entire bible and I couldn't believe that with everything that he taught he failed to mention the most important thing in all of Scripture. He failed to see the most important thing Jesus is and came to reveal; "the Life was the light of men." What do I mean?

The beginning of the bible starts with God presenting Himself to us as the Tree of Life (Genesis 2:9) and the bible ends with the tree of Life in New Jerusalem (Revelation 22). Adam's curse is the loss of Life (Genesis 2:17).

Jesus tells us that He came to give us Life (John 10:10).

Jesus tells us that He is that Life (John 1:4).

He tells us that whoever receives Him will receive Life (John 5:24).

The central issue of the bible is not that man is bad, but that man is dead (Ephesians 2:1).

The critical issue of all is the reception is Christ as Life (1 John 5:12).

The moment He touches us we instantaneously understand that He is all we have, ever really wanted and the only thing we will ever need (John 14.6).

This reveals to us that He alone is the Life, that we do not possess anything apart from receiving Him (John 6:53).

We must continually receive Him as our Life-supply (John 6:57).

Tozer's words are still true today, "That kind of Christianity that relies upon the influence of its own human and earthly power makes God sick…" There exists no more certain cause of Spiritual degeneration than the neglect of taking time to receive His Life, all by yourself. The problem today is not a lack of work but a lack of LIFE. But without receiving life through enjoyment there is no abiding fruit. Jesus teaches us in John 14, the principle of the "Vine and branches" - The branches receive life though the vine and effortlessly fruit is born. Robert Murray McCheyne wrote, "If you will come to Jesus and drink, you shall become a fountain of grace to your family."

All that I wish to convey through this book is that the lovesick life lives touching the living Christ and as a result, it reveals the living Christ.

Dear reader, His hand is outstretched waiting to melt our hearts with His tender touch, we just need to sit down and quietly give our souls up to Him. Oh to sum up the lovesick life – with His presence, everything is right. Without His presence, everything is wrong. Everything depends on His presence.

Appendix

"…He who eats Me will live because of Me…"
John 6:57

We are far more interested in the enduring than we are the immediate. What does that mean? We want to see things endure and not just happen. It's one thing for a thing to take place, it's another thing for it to withstand the test of time and the fires of life.

I've said this, written this, and proclaimed this before, and I'll repeat it till the day I die: unless the public touch becomes a private kiss, our accumulative experience in God will fade away. A public touch will happen if you avail yourself to meetings. A private kiss will happen if you avail yourself to Him. That private kiss will solidify your experience and knowing of Jesus and cause what you've gained in God to endure.

In the midst of the 66 books of the Bible, one book stands in a category of its own. There is not another like it. It's the Song of Solomon. It's the clearest word-picture that we have of a relationship with Jesus. It paints so clearly with words the intimate romance of a life lived in the affection of God. It's even more clear than a parable. It's a stage set and story told with vivid imagery that expresses the heart of God. The Lord literally chose to display a picture of His romantic function in your heart with this book.

Consider it, the fact that there is a romance in the center of the scriptures is revealing to us that this is what God wants us to feel with Him. Hudson Taylor said this about the book: "Song of Solomon is the divine warrant for the desire for sensible manifestations of His presence."

What does that mean? The poetic masterpiece of love that we read about, the mutual exchange of love is Christianity. Christianity isn't a relationship with a book or collection of spiritual data. It's a living exchange involving actual manifestations between the Lover and the beloved.

If there is one thing that I get hit with in e-mails and by internet trolls more than anything, it's that I preach and emphasize experience far too much. Yet Song of Solomon destroys all of the arguments! This book continually pours out word-pictures blasting a loud and clear message that God is experiential. It describes God as having honey dripping from His lips! It doesn't say, "He has calloused data flowing from His mouth." He isn't a boring lover! Fire, water, light, honey, wine… all descriptions of the person of God throughout the thread of scripture, yet somehow we say He can't be felt. He is trying to tell us something. What is that something? "Taste Me! Touch Me! Experience Me! Know Me!"

The Shulamite Bride said, "Your love is better than wine." Wine is tasted, then it's received, and then it causes influence. She was inebriated with his very person. I once met a woman in Arizona who had been battered by past relationships. So much abuse and heartache had wreaked havoc on her connections with men. She came to Christ and wanted to remarry, and one day looked up to the Lord uncertainly, and asked, "Lord, who will want me?" She heard the voice of the Lord say, "Marry me!"

That is the root of what God is wanting! A people who will leap at the opportunity to experience His romantic love.

If you know anything about Jesus and walk with Him for any period of time, you know that He is distinctly romantic. God has a way of sweeping us away to experience sights, sounds, and smells of His presence and character. Suddenly, we find ourselves reminded of His sweetness and longing for more of Him.

When I was in the Brownsville revival, they used a very distinct air freshener in the church. Up until that point, I had never experienced that smell before, and for years and years after, I never experienced it again, until recently.

We went into an Italian restaurant and as soon as I walked into the restroom, I smelled the same exact air freshener from years ago at Brownsville! I immediately fell to my knees and said, "I remember, Lord! I will not forget what You did for me. I won't forget how You kissed me.

I'll live for you all of my days wholeheartedly." It's as if the Lord brings these things back up just to remind us of our affection for Him and His affection for us.

Within the stand-out book of the Song of Solomon, I believe there is a stand-out word.

To me, it sums up the entire book. It's found in the fifth verse of the second chapter. What is that word? Lovesick. It was declared, "I am lovesick." This word is God's word, not man's word. What a word! I don't know another like it. The word itself seems to evoke feeling. Two words that are seemingly opposites — love and sick — yet somehow are perfectly harmonious.

It connotes a reality that a love so strong can be felt physically. This word is God's chosen language to describe His relationship with the bride. It's almost a hyperbole. A hyperbole is an exaggerated statement used to make a point.

He is seeking to communicate to us the height of love! The early church had a phrase which was similar called "the wounded heart." It was the idea that a heart would be gashed when coming in direct contact with God. In this, the heart bleeds and throbs with longing for the person of Jesus.

Every lull in the midst of your day is an invitation to come away. The lovesick one says, "I feel a vulnerability like one who has been wounded severely and my only safety is to remain near you."

David took a shot at expressing this feeling of lovesickness by saying, "My soul pines for You." What does it mean to pine? It means to suffer out of desire. It's a longing so deep that pain is involved! Listen, this isn't just for the select few. Whether you're in middle school, college, or something else; whether you're a stay at home mom or a real estate investor — this is for you! It's the life we're all called to live.

In Ezekiel 26:36, the Lord describes His process of removing a stony, hard heart of flesh and replacing it with a soft heart of flesh. In other words, God is replacing our old hearts with one that is able to love Him! It's a heart that is capable of feeling the affection of God and walking in His ways.

David Brainard wrote in his journal, "Oh this pleasing pain that makes my soul look for God." An early church writer once wrote, "Oh sweetness and beauty everlasting, you have wounded my heart and I'm scarcely alive for I die in the face of your joy."

Early church writers developed a word called epekatsis. It's literally a word they made up in an attempt to describe the sensation in the soul when one is blissfully satisfied in Him yet completely longing and burning for more. It's a sort of tearing in the heart.

My favorite expression to describe lovesickness is the term "the lover's ache." It's the pleasurable satisfaction of God combined with an aching for increase.

The Bible says that the love of God is shed abroad in our hearts by the Holy Ghost (see Romans 5:5). It's a literal eruption. I remember when I first began experiencing this. Something caught my eye in the first chapter of Song of Songs. She said, "Kiss me with the kisses of your mouth" (Song of Solomon 1:2). Then in chapter two, she says, "I am lovesick" (Song of Solomon 2:5).

I figure, if she is kissed in chapter one and lovesick by chapter two, then this must be a sickness caught by kisses! He spreads the sickness of love throughout the world by kissing people. Once you've been kissed by God, you cannot live unless you're kissed again! May His kiss be continually upon our lives! I often wake up in my room and rest my head against the headboard and say, "Oh Lord, even as yesterday, kiss me again that I may go on living." It's the kiss that kills the old man. It's an infection of affection!

Gordon Fee once wrote, "When a man receives the Holy Spirit, divine perfection does not set in but divine infection does."

There is no softer heart than one that lives in the kisses of God. See, this sort of language bothers some people. I would say that you misunderstand His nature. You cannot read the book of Song of Solomon with a pure heart without coming to the conclusion that these descriptors are so very accurate in detailing our King.

When the infection of lovesickness entered my being, I didn't know exactly what was happening to me; however, I longed for more. In fact, I had such a deep desire for solitude. As did the Shulamite Bride. She said, "Meet me in the clefs of the rock in the steep pathway, all alone" (Song of Solomon 2:14).

Lovers love to be alone. They instinctively seek retreat. A retreat in which no other voice is heard and no other face is seen. A retreat in which the sights and sounds thrill the soul like nothing else. This is what He wants with you. You have to receive the love of God continually so that you can love God back continually.

It's the kiss of God that creates the bride. It's only the kiss that can make a singled eye. See, the kiss is your cure! The kiss is your call! His kiss can cure your evil and bring you into bliss! His kiss connects you back to the one for whom you sigh. There is an infection of affection for you!

The kiss kills so much darkness in the heart of men. You become His lips for mankind by being kissed by them. In Song of Solomon 2:5, we see that she says, "refresh me, for I am lovesick!" This displays that she was continually going to him for refreshment! In other words, "Without you I quickly grow stale!"

If you know anything about spirituality, you know that so quickly staleness can set into the heart! Everything might look the same on the outside. You might have the same look, the same talk, and the same exterior, yet you know that a staleness has developed in your spirit. Your call is to turn back to the reviver! Turn back to the refresher! Many people are crying out for revival, yet He is the revival!

The bride is showing us that the kiss will infect you with a lovesickness that causes you to call out for continual refreshment. People around you, in time, will begin to see that staleness will lead you into death.

Those who walked away from God did so because they first became stale. They first became stale because they stopped receiving the kisses of God. Staleness causes us to lose touch with the reality that His lips drip with honey.

The bride goes on to say, "Sustain me for I am lovesick" (Song of Solomon 2:5). She is looking to be upheld by the groom. She is looking to him for continual keeping. She essentially says, "You've got to keep me for I cannot keep myself!"

These are the symptoms of lovesickness. Lord, keep us for we cannot keep ourselves! Sustain us, God, for we cannot sustain ourselves! May an addiction to the kisses of God be birthed within us. May we be chained to the person of Jesus by our desire-filled clinging.

The bride's dependency is built on lovesickness. She is so taken with him that she is no longer the same person. We were lost before His kiss… and now we are lost without His kisses. Before He kissed us, we were completely lost. We have grown into a helpless addiction to God… and this helplessness is our safety.

Do you know how to reach safety? Dependency. The lovesickness longs for direct contact. In the next verse, she says, "Let his left hand be under my head And his right hand embrace me" (Song of Solomon 2:6). She wants to be held by him. She isn't content by being merely where he is. She wants direct contact with him. May the Lord hold us and drain us of our inward poisons.

Charles Spurgeon said, "He kills your doubts and your fears by the closeness of His embrace." Sometimes the greatest thing God can say to us is not intelligible at all, it's simply being held.

Sometimes in my day when things get rough and I feel bombarded, I'll just stop where I am and cry out, "Hold me, Lord. You know me and I need Thee. Hold me, Lord." Our greatest need sometimes is not to know, it's to feel. We need to feel His nearness. I'd rather be able to feel sickness of love than to define it.

According to the dictionary, lovesickness means to be so in love that one is unable to act normally. Don't you know that this is our call? A behavior modification brought about through the intoxication of love. "If you love Me, you will keep My commandments" (John 14:15). Can you imagine Jesus standing before His beloved disciples and saying, "If you fall in love with Me, obeying Me will come naturally"? As we fall in love with Him, He takes us into His arms and performs obedience through us.

Obedience is a proof of love only because obedience is the nature of love. St. John of the Cross said, "If one walks lovesick before God He fulfills the commandment of God to perfection." Only if our lives are taken with Him can they be truly unto Him.

There is a fictional story that says the Apostles had seen Jesus in His fullness and His awesome power. They watched and marveled as He spoke and acted — full of God, for He was God. They ran to get Nathanael and longed to introduce Nathanael to Jesus. As they went on the way, Nathanael said, "What is He like?" Peter said, "His face was so, so powerful." John said, "No, no, no, it was His voice. His voice was so rich." Then James interjected and said, "We don't know what it was… we just know that He is magical." They didn't have any words to describe Him. Nathanael shot back, "I don't believe in magic."

John replied, "Oh, you will when you see Him." See, every time I see Him, I am convicted of forgetting how beautiful He really is. When you see Him, yes, He will captivate your heart, yet His character is of such a variety that you could fall in love with Him with your eyes closed! God's design was never to corner men and collect their consent, but rather to captivate their hearts by displaying the beauty of His own nature!

Lovesickness causes us to act differently. Lovesick ones look strange to those who aren't infected. I remember being in London waiting for someone to get through customs. As a group of us waited for those who were coming, a girl ran toward a man who came through the entryway. They began kissing and embracing. I was amazed because they didn't seem to want to stop. I laughingly almost wondered how far this was going to go, as it bordered on uncomfortable. They didn't care who was around or what they looked like. They were lovesick and focused solely on each other, and not on the crowd.

When you're lovesick toward God, you don't care about those in the room. You just want kiss upon kiss from the Lord. The lovesick forsake others to keep close to the One for whom they love. When you've tasted Him, you lose taste for everything else. When you've tasted Him, you lose taste for the world. God Himself is the maximum delight of the universe. The chief aim of man is to glorify God by finding pleasure in Him. The sum of Christianity is not behave, but behold. To see Him is to fall in love with Him.

Shakespeare once said, "Journeys end in lovers meeting." A.W. Tozer expounded on this saying, "A man who has met God is not looking for anything because he has found it!" Competition, comparison, relevance, and a need for significance… all things that plague the human psyche, yet all things that are killed with a kiss. Shakespeare also dropped another phrase concerning love.

He said, "A lover's eyes will gaze an eagle blind." What does it mean? I don't know, but it sounds like when you're lovesick, you are fixed upon Him. All of the problems that you have are a deviated gaze. Ten degrees off today is a mile tomorrow. Thus, we must be captivated by Him everyday.

So many are not wrapped in the enjoyment of God because they're tied down by all of the things they want from Him. I pray that lovesickness would come upon you. I pray that you'd be brought to a place in which you say, "You are here, Lord… what more could I want?" If I were a counselor and you came to me with a million problems, I would respond by simply asking, "When was your last kiss?"

Why? Because the kiss of God solves and dissolves so many of our problems. He is so available! You can have as many kisses as you want. Tozer said, "Let no man say he wants more of God because if he wanted more of God he would get more of God because He gives Himself freely to all."

If there is no kiss, it's because you don't want it. The Lord is already leaning from heaven ready to kiss you. It's why the bride didn't say, "I'm going to kiss him" but instead, "let him kiss me!" You may say, "I've been struggling." I'm here to tell you, His kiss is your cure. His kiss is the bliss of life no matter your situation. It transcends your circumstances.

The Hebrew word for worship points to the word kiss. The secret to experience the kiss of God is worship. Turn your heart toward Him. Let Him embrace you. Let the kiss of His presence fill you and encounter you, as you encounter Him.

About the Author

Eric William Gilmour is the founder of Sonship International — a ministry seeking to bring the church into a deeper experience of God's presence in their daily lives. He enjoys writing on the revelation of Jesus Christ in the Scriptures and personal experience of God. He lives in Florida with his wife Brooke and their two daughters.

MORE FROM ERIC GILMOUR

available on amazon.com

SONSHIP-INTERNATIONAL.COM

Lovesick: The Longing of the Bride

Pulpit to Page Publishing Co.
USA & ABROAD
pulpittopage.com

CPSIA information can be obtained
at www.ICGtesting.com
Printed in the USA
LVHW04*1557061018
592662LV00002B/5/P